50 Autumn Abundance Recipes for Home

By: Kelly Johnson

Table of Contents

- Pumpkin Pancakes
- Carrot Cake Muffins
- Roasted Fennel and Citrus Salad
- Harvest Quinoa Salad
- Mulled Apple Cider
- Sweet Potato Casserole
- Spaghetti Squash Primavera
- Maple Pecan Granola
- Pumpkin Seed Pesto
- Chocolate Chip Pumpkin Bread
- Roasted Garlic and Rosemary Mashed Potatoes
- Acorn Squash and Wild Rice Soup
- Honeycrisp Apple Salad
- Maple Dijon Glazed Salmon
- Chocolate Hazelnut Spread with Apples

Pumpkin Spice Soup

Ingredients

- 2 tablespoons olive oil
- 1 medium onion, diced
- 2 cloves garlic, minced
- 1 tablespoon fresh ginger, grated
- 1 teaspoon ground cumin
- 1 teaspoon ground cinnamon
- ½ teaspoon nutmeg
- ½ teaspoon allspice
- 1 (15 oz) can pumpkin puree (or about 2 cups fresh pumpkin, cooked and pureed)
- 4 cups vegetable broth
- 1 cup coconut milk (or heavy cream for a richer soup)
- Salt and pepper to taste
- Optional toppings:
  - Pumpkin seeds
  - A dollop of yogurt or sour cream
  - Fresh herbs (like cilantro or parsley)

Instructions

1. **Sauté the Aromatics**: In a large pot, heat the olive oil over medium heat. Add the diced onion and sauté until translucent, about 5 minutes. Stir in the garlic and ginger, cooking for another 1-2 minutes until fragrant.
2. **Add the Spices**: Sprinkle in the cumin, cinnamon, nutmeg, and allspice. Stir well, allowing the spices to toast for about 1 minute.
3. **Incorporate Pumpkin**: Add the pumpkin puree, mixing it thoroughly with the sautéed vegetables and spices.
4. **Pour in Broth**: Gradually add the vegetable broth, stirring to combine. Bring the mixture to a gentle simmer, and let it cook for about 15 minutes, allowing the flavors to meld.
5. **Blend**: Use an immersion blender to purée the soup until smooth. Alternatively, transfer the soup in batches to a blender, then return it to the pot.
6. **Add Creaminess**: Stir in the coconut milk (or heavy cream) and heat through. Adjust the seasoning with salt and pepper to taste.

7. **Serve**: Ladle the soup into bowls and top with pumpkin seeds, a dollop of yogurt, or fresh herbs, if desired.

Enjoy!

This Pumpkin Spice Soup is perfect as a starter or a light meal paired with crusty bread. Its rich flavors and creamy texture will have you reaching for seconds!

Roasted Butternut Squash Salad

Ingredients

- 1 medium butternut squash, peeled and cubed
- 2 tablespoons olive oil
- Salt and pepper to taste
- 5 cups mixed greens
- ½ cup feta cheese, crumbled
- ¼ cup dried cranberries
- ¼ cup walnuts, toasted
- Balsamic vinaigrette for dressing

Instructions

1. Preheat the oven to 400°F (200°C). Toss the butternut squash with olive oil, salt, and pepper. Spread on a baking sheet and roast for 25-30 minutes, or until tender.
2. In a large bowl, combine mixed greens, roasted squash, feta, cranberries, and walnuts.
3. Drizzle with balsamic vinaigrette and toss to combine. Serve immediately.

Apple Cider Braised Pork

Ingredients

- 2 lbs pork shoulder, cut into chunks
- Salt and pepper to taste
- 2 tablespoons olive oil
- 1 onion, diced
- 3 cloves garlic, minced
- 2 cups apple cider
- 1 tablespoon fresh thyme
- 1 tablespoon Dijon mustard
- 1 tablespoon apple cider vinegar

Instructions

1. Season pork with salt and pepper. In a large pot, heat olive oil over medium-high heat. Sear pork until browned on all sides. Remove and set aside.
2. In the same pot, add onion and garlic, cooking until softened.
3. Return pork to the pot and add apple cider, thyme, mustard, and vinegar. Bring to a simmer.
4. Cover and braise in a 325°F (160°C) oven for 2-3 hours, until tender. Serve with the braising liquid.

Maple Glazed Brussels Sprouts

Ingredients

- 1 lb Brussels sprouts, halved
- 2 tablespoons olive oil
- ¼ cup maple syrup
- Salt and pepper to taste

Instructions

1. Preheat oven to 400°F (200°C). Toss Brussels sprouts with olive oil, maple syrup, salt, and pepper.
2. Spread on a baking sheet and roast for 20-25 minutes, until caramelized and tender. Serve warm.

Sweet Potato and Black Bean Chili

Ingredients

- 1 tablespoon olive oil
- 1 onion, diced
- 2 cloves garlic, minced
- 1 bell pepper, diced
- 2 medium sweet potatoes, peeled and cubed
- 1 can (15 oz) black beans, drained and rinsed
- 1 can (14 oz) diced tomatoes
- 2 cups vegetable broth
- 1 tablespoon chili powder
- 1 teaspoon cumin
- Salt and pepper to taste

Instructions

1. In a large pot, heat olive oil over medium heat. Sauté onion, garlic, and bell pepper until softened.
2. Add sweet potatoes, black beans, tomatoes, broth, chili powder, cumin, salt, and pepper. Bring to a boil, then reduce heat and simmer for 25-30 minutes, until sweet potatoes are tender. Serve hot.

Pear and Gorgonzola Tart

Ingredients

- 1 sheet puff pastry, thawed
- 2 ripe pears, thinly sliced
- ½ cup Gorgonzola cheese, crumbled
- 2 tablespoons honey
- Fresh thyme for garnish (optional)

Instructions

1. Preheat oven to 400°F (200°C). Roll out puff pastry on a baking sheet.
2. Arrange pear slices on the pastry, leaving a border. Sprinkle with Gorgonzola and drizzle with honey.
3. Bake for 20-25 minutes, until pastry is golden. Garnish with fresh thyme before serving.

Cranberry Orange Scones

Ingredients

- 2 cups all-purpose flour
- ¼ cup sugar
- 1 tablespoon baking powder
- ½ teaspoon salt
- ½ cup cold butter, cubed
- ¾ cup dried cranberries
- Zest of 1 orange
- ½ cup heavy cream
- 1 large egg

Instructions

1. Preheat oven to 400°F (200°C). In a bowl, mix flour, sugar, baking powder, and salt. Cut in butter until mixture resembles coarse crumbs.
2. Stir in cranberries and orange zest. In another bowl, whisk together cream and egg. Add to dry ingredients and mix until just combined.
3. Turn dough onto a floured surface and shape into a circle. Cut into wedges and place on a baking sheet. Bake for 15-20 minutes until golden.

Mushroom Risotto with Thyme

Ingredients

- 1 tablespoon olive oil
- 1 onion, finely chopped
- 2 cups arborio rice
- 4 cups vegetable broth
- 1 cup mushrooms, sliced
- ½ cup white wine (optional)
- 1 teaspoon fresh thyme
- ½ cup Parmesan cheese, grated
- Salt and pepper to taste

Instructions

1. In a saucepan, heat broth and keep warm. In a large skillet, heat olive oil. Sauté onion until translucent.
2. Add mushrooms and thyme, cooking until mushrooms are soft. Stir in arborio rice, cooking for 2 minutes.
3. Add white wine, if using, and cook until absorbed. Gradually add warm broth, one ladle at a time, stirring continuously until absorbed before adding more. Cook for about 20 minutes until creamy.
4. Stir in Parmesan, and season with salt and pepper. Serve immediately.

Stuffed Acorn Squash

Ingredients

- 2 acorn squash, halved and seeded
- 1 tablespoon olive oil
- 1 cup quinoa, cooked
- 1 cup black beans, drained and rinsed
- 1 cup corn (fresh or frozen)
- 1 teaspoon cumin
- Salt and pepper to taste
- ½ cup cheese (cheddar or feta), optional

Instructions

1. Preheat oven to 400°F (200°C). Brush acorn squash halves with olive oil and season with salt and pepper. Place cut-side down on a baking sheet and roast for 25-30 minutes.
2. In a bowl, combine cooked quinoa, black beans, corn, cumin, salt, and pepper.
3. Remove squash from the oven, flip them cut-side up, and fill each half with the quinoa mixture. Top with cheese, if desired.
4. Return to the oven and bake for an additional 10-15 minutes. Serve warm.

Spiced Apple Crisp

Ingredients

- 4 cups apples, peeled and sliced
- 1 cup brown sugar
- 1 teaspoon cinnamon
- ½ teaspoon nutmeg
- 1 tablespoon lemon juice
- 1 cup rolled oats
- 1 cup all-purpose flour
- ½ cup butter, softened
- ½ cup granola (optional)

Instructions

1. Preheat oven to 350°F (175°C). In a bowl, toss apples with lemon juice, brown sugar, cinnamon, and nutmeg. Place in a greased 9x13 inch baking dish.
2. In another bowl, mix oats, flour, and butter until crumbly. Sprinkle over apples. If using, add granola on top.
3. Bake for 30-35 minutes until golden and bubbly. Serve warm, optionally with vanilla ice cream.

Autumn Vegetable Gratin

Ingredients

- 2 cups butternut squash, sliced
- 2 cups zucchini, sliced
- 2 cups potatoes, sliced
- 1 onion, thinly sliced
- 2 cups shredded cheese (Gruyère or cheddar)
- 1 cup heavy cream
- 2 tablespoons olive oil
- Salt and pepper to taste
- 1 teaspoon thyme

Instructions

1. Preheat oven to 375°F (190°C). Grease a baking dish. Layer butternut squash, zucchini, potatoes, and onion in the dish, seasoning each layer with salt, pepper, and thyme.
2. Pour heavy cream over the top and sprinkle cheese evenly.
3. Drizzle olive oil over the top. Cover with foil and bake for 45 minutes. Remove foil and bake for an additional 15-20 minutes until golden.

Butternut Squash Risotto

Ingredients

- 1 cup arborio rice
- 2 cups butternut squash, diced
- 1 onion, finely chopped
- 2 cloves garlic, minced
- 4 cups vegetable broth
- 1 cup white wine (optional)
- ½ cup Parmesan cheese, grated
- 2 tablespoons olive oil
- Salt and pepper to taste
- Fresh sage for garnish (optional)

Instructions

1. In a saucepan, heat broth and keep warm. In a large skillet, heat olive oil. Sauté onion and garlic until soft.
2. Add butternut squash and cook for 5 minutes. Stir in arborio rice and cook for 2 minutes.
3. Add white wine, if using, and stir until absorbed. Gradually add warm broth, one ladle at a time, stirring continuously until absorbed. Cook for about 20 minutes until creamy.
4. Stir in Parmesan, salt, and pepper. Garnish with fresh sage, if desired.

Caramelized Onion and Pumpkin Quiche

Ingredients

- 1 pie crust (store-bought or homemade)
- 2 cups pumpkin puree
- 2 onions, sliced
- 3 eggs
- 1 cup heavy cream
- 1 teaspoon thyme
- Salt and pepper to taste
- 1 cup cheese (feta or goat cheese), crumbled

Instructions

1. Preheat oven to 375°F (190°C). In a skillet, caramelize onions over medium heat until golden and soft.
2. In a bowl, whisk together pumpkin puree, eggs, heavy cream, thyme, salt, and pepper.
3. Spread caramelized onions in the pie crust, pour pumpkin mixture over, and top with cheese.
4. Bake for 40-45 minutes until set and golden. Let cool before slicing.

Chestnut and Wild Rice Pilaf

Ingredients

- 1 cup wild rice
- 2 cups vegetable broth
- 1 cup chestnuts, cooked and chopped
- 1 onion, diced
- 2 cloves garlic, minced
- 2 tablespoons olive oil
- 1 teaspoon thyme
- Salt and pepper to taste
- ¼ cup parsley, chopped (for garnish)

Instructions

1. In a pot, heat olive oil. Sauté onion and garlic until soft. Add wild rice and stir for 2 minutes.
2. Pour in vegetable broth and bring to a boil. Reduce heat, cover, and simmer for 45 minutes until rice is tender.
3. Stir in chestnuts, thyme, salt, and pepper. Cook for an additional 5 minutes. Garnish with parsley before serving.

Maple Roasted Carrots

Ingredients

- 1 lb carrots, peeled and cut into sticks
- 2 tablespoons olive oil
- ¼ cup maple syrup
- Salt and pepper to taste
- Fresh thyme for garnish (optional)

Instructions

1. Preheat oven to 400°F (200°C). Toss carrots with olive oil, maple syrup, salt, and pepper.
2. Spread on a baking sheet and roast for 25-30 minutes, until caramelized and tender. Garnish with fresh thyme before serving.

Pear and Walnut Salad

Ingredients

- 4 cups mixed greens
- 2 ripe pears, sliced
- ½ cup walnuts, toasted
- ½ cup crumbled blue cheese (or feta)
- ¼ cup balsamic vinaigrette

Instructions

1. In a large bowl, combine mixed greens, pear slices, walnuts, and cheese.
2. Drizzle with balsamic vinaigrette and toss gently. Serve immediately.

Pumpkin Cheesecake Bars

Ingredients

- 1 cup graham cracker crumbs
- ½ cup butter, melted
- 2 cups cream cheese, softened
- 1 cup pumpkin puree
- ¾ cup sugar
- 3 eggs
- 1 teaspoon vanilla extract
- 1 teaspoon cinnamon

Instructions

1. Preheat oven to 350°F (175°C). In a bowl, mix graham cracker crumbs and melted butter. Press into the bottom of a greased baking dish.
2. In another bowl, beat cream cheese until smooth. Add pumpkin, sugar, eggs, vanilla, and cinnamon. Mix until combined.
3. Pour filling over the crust and bake for 30-35 minutes, until set. Cool before slicing into bars.

Cinnamon Sugar Roasted Chickpeas

Ingredients

- 1 can (15 oz) chickpeas, drained and rinsed
- 1 tablespoon olive oil
- 2 tablespoons sugar
- 1 teaspoon cinnamon
- Pinch of salt

Instructions

1. Preheat oven to 400°F (200°C). Pat chickpeas dry with a towel.
2. Toss chickpeas with olive oil, sugar, cinnamon, and salt. Spread on a baking sheet.
3. Roast for 25-30 minutes, stirring occasionally, until crispy. Let cool before serving.

Harvest Grain Bowl

Ingredients

- 1 cup cooked quinoa or farro
- 1 cup roasted sweet potatoes, cubed
- 1 cup kale or spinach, wilted
- ½ cup chickpeas, roasted
- ½ avocado, sliced
- ¼ cup dried cranberries
- ¼ cup feta cheese, crumbled (optional)
- 2 tablespoons olive oil
- 1 tablespoon balsamic vinegar
- Salt and pepper to taste

Instructions

1. In a large bowl, combine quinoa, roasted sweet potatoes, kale, chickpeas, and cranberries.
2. Drizzle with olive oil and balsamic vinegar, then toss to combine. Season with salt and pepper.
3. Top with sliced avocado and feta cheese, if using. Serve immediately.

Spiced Pecan Pie

Ingredients

- 1 ½ cups pecans, chopped
- 1 cup light corn syrup
- ¾ cup brown sugar
- ½ cup granulated sugar
- 3 large eggs
- ¼ cup melted butter
- 1 teaspoon vanilla extract
- 1 teaspoon cinnamon
- ½ teaspoon nutmeg
- 1 pie crust (store-bought or homemade)

Instructions

1. Preheat oven to 350°F (175°C). Fit the pie crust into a pie dish.
2. In a large bowl, mix corn syrup, brown sugar, granulated sugar, eggs, melted butter, vanilla, cinnamon, and nutmeg.
3. Stir in chopped pecans, then pour filling into the pie crust.
4. Bake for 50-60 minutes, until set. Let cool before serving.

Beet and Goat Cheese Salad

Ingredients

- 2 cups mixed greens
- 2 cups roasted beets, sliced
- ½ cup goat cheese, crumbled
- ¼ cup walnuts, toasted
- 2 tablespoons balsamic vinaigrette
- Salt and pepper to taste

Instructions

1. In a large bowl, combine mixed greens, roasted beets, goat cheese, and walnuts.
2. Drizzle with balsamic vinaigrette and toss gently. Season with salt and pepper to taste. Serve immediately.

Sage Brown Butter Pasta

Ingredients

- 8 oz pasta (like fettuccine or pappardelle)
- ½ cup unsalted butter
- 10-12 fresh sage leaves
- ¼ cup grated Parmesan cheese
- Salt and pepper to taste

Instructions

1. Cook pasta according to package instructions. Drain and set aside.
2. In a skillet, melt butter over medium heat. Add sage leaves and cook until butter turns golden brown and sage is crispy, about 3-4 minutes.
3. Toss cooked pasta in the brown butter, then stir in Parmesan, salt, and pepper. Serve warm.

Honey Glazed Sweet Potatoes

Ingredients

- 2 lbs sweet potatoes, peeled and cubed
- 3 tablespoons olive oil
- ¼ cup honey
- Salt and pepper to taste
- 1 teaspoon cinnamon (optional)

Instructions

1. Preheat oven to 400°F (200°C). Toss sweet potatoes with olive oil, honey, salt, pepper, and cinnamon (if using).
2. Spread on a baking sheet and roast for 25-30 minutes, until tender and caramelized. Serve warm.

Cranberry Walnut Bread

Ingredients

- 2 cups all-purpose flour
- 1 cup whole wheat flour
- 1 cup sugar
- 1 teaspoon baking soda
- ½ teaspoon salt
- 1 cup chopped walnuts
- 1 cup dried cranberries
- 2 large eggs
- 1 cup orange juice
- ½ cup vegetable oil

Instructions

1. Preheat oven to 350°F (175°C). Grease a loaf pan.
2. In a large bowl, combine flours, sugar, baking soda, salt, walnuts, and cranberries.
3. In another bowl, whisk together eggs, orange juice, and oil. Pour wet ingredients into dry ingredients and mix until just combined.
4. Pour batter into the prepared loaf pan and bake for 60-70 minutes, until a toothpick comes out clean. Let cool before slicing.

Curried Pumpkin Hummus

Ingredients

- 1 can (15 oz) chickpeas, drained and rinsed
- 1 cup pumpkin puree
- 2 tablespoons tahini
- 1 tablespoon olive oil
- 1 tablespoon lemon juice
- 1 teaspoon curry powder
- Salt and pepper to taste
- Water as needed for consistency

Instructions

1. In a food processor, combine chickpeas, pumpkin puree, tahini, olive oil, lemon juice, curry powder, salt, and pepper.
2. Blend until smooth, adding water as needed to reach desired consistency. Serve with pita chips or veggies.

Maple Cinnamon Oatmeal

Ingredients

- 1 cup rolled oats
- 2 cups water or milk
- 2 tablespoons maple syrup
- 1 teaspoon cinnamon
- Pinch of salt
- Toppings (e.g., sliced bananas, nuts, dried fruits)

Instructions

1. In a pot, combine oats, water (or milk), maple syrup, cinnamon, and salt. Bring to a boil.
2. Reduce heat and simmer for 5-7 minutes until oats are cooked. Stir occasionally.
3. Serve warm, topped with your choice of fruits and nuts.

Roasted Apple and Squash Soup

Ingredients

- 1 medium butternut squash, peeled and cubed
- 2 apples, cored and chopped
- 1 onion, chopped
- 2 cloves garlic, minced
- 4 cups vegetable broth
- 2 tablespoons olive oil
- 1 teaspoon cinnamon
- Salt and pepper to taste

Instructions

1. Preheat oven to 400°F (200°C). Toss squash, apples, onion, and garlic with olive oil, cinnamon, salt, and pepper. Spread on a baking sheet and roast for 25-30 minutes until tender.
2. In a pot, combine roasted vegetables and broth. Bring to a simmer, then blend until smooth.
3. Serve warm, garnished with a drizzle of olive oil or a sprinkle of cinnamon.

Pomegranate Glazed Brussels Sprouts

Ingredients

- 1 lb Brussels sprouts, halved
- 2 tablespoons olive oil
- Salt and pepper to taste
- ½ cup pomegranate seeds
- ¼ cup balsamic vinegar
- 2 tablespoons honey

Instructions

1. Preheat oven to 400°F (200°C). Toss Brussels sprouts with olive oil, salt, and pepper, and spread them on a baking sheet.
2. Roast for 20-25 minutes until caramelized and tender.
3. In a small saucepan, combine balsamic vinegar and honey, bringing to a simmer until slightly thickened.
4. Drizzle the glaze over roasted Brussels sprouts and toss with pomegranate seeds. Serve warm.

Autumn Harvest Tacos

Ingredients

- 8 corn tortillas
- 1 cup roasted sweet potatoes, cubed
- 1 cup black beans, drained and rinsed
- ½ cup corn (fresh or frozen)
- 1 avocado, sliced
- ¼ cup feta cheese, crumbled (optional)
- 1 teaspoon cumin
- Salt and pepper to taste
- Fresh cilantro for garnish

Instructions

1. In a bowl, combine roasted sweet potatoes, black beans, corn, cumin, salt, and pepper.
2. Warm corn tortillas in a skillet or microwave.
3. Assemble tacos by placing the mixture on each tortilla, topping with avocado, feta, and cilantro. Serve immediately.

Gingerbread Pancakes

Ingredients

- 1 cup all-purpose flour
- 2 tablespoons brown sugar
- 1 teaspoon baking powder
- ½ teaspoon baking soda
- 1 teaspoon ginger
- 1 teaspoon cinnamon
- ¼ teaspoon nutmeg
- ¼ teaspoon salt
- 1 cup buttermilk
- 1 large egg
- 2 tablespoons molasses
- 2 tablespoons melted butter

Instructions

1. In a large bowl, whisk together flour, brown sugar, baking powder, baking soda, ginger, cinnamon, nutmeg, and salt.
2. In another bowl, mix buttermilk, egg, molasses, and melted butter. Combine wet and dry ingredients until just mixed.
3. Heat a non-stick skillet over medium heat. Pour ¼ cup of batter for each pancake, cooking until bubbles form, then flip and cook until golden. Serve with syrup.

Spiced Roasted Cauliflower

Ingredients

- 1 head cauliflower, cut into florets
- 2 tablespoons olive oil
- 1 teaspoon cumin
- 1 teaspoon paprika
- 1 teaspoon garlic powder
- Salt and pepper to taste
- Fresh parsley for garnish

Instructions

1. Preheat oven to 425°F (220°C). Toss cauliflower florets with olive oil, cumin, paprika, garlic powder, salt, and pepper.
2. Spread on a baking sheet and roast for 25-30 minutes until golden and tender.
3. Garnish with fresh parsley before serving.

Creamy Mushroom Soup

Ingredients

- 2 cups mushrooms, sliced
- 1 onion, diced
- 2 cloves garlic, minced
- 4 cups vegetable broth
- 1 cup heavy cream
- 2 tablespoons olive oil
- 1 tablespoon thyme
- Salt and pepper to taste

Instructions

1. In a pot, heat olive oil over medium heat. Sauté onion and garlic until softened.
2. Add mushrooms and thyme, cooking until mushrooms are browned.
3. Pour in vegetable broth and bring to a simmer for 15 minutes.
4. Blend until smooth, then stir in heavy cream. Season with salt and pepper, and serve warm.

Nutty Granola Bars

Ingredients

- 2 cups rolled oats
- ½ cup almond butter
- ½ cup honey or maple syrup
- 1 cup mixed nuts (almonds, walnuts, pecans), chopped
- ½ cup dried fruit (cranberries, apricots, etc.)
- 1 teaspoon vanilla extract
- Pinch of salt

Instructions

1. Preheat oven to 350°F (175°C). Line an 8x8 inch baking dish with parchment paper.
2. In a bowl, mix oats, almond butter, honey, nuts, dried fruit, vanilla, and salt until well combined.
3. Press the mixture into the prepared baking dish. Bake for 20-25 minutes until golden.
4. Allow to cool completely before cutting into bars.

Harvest Vegetable Curry

Ingredients

- 2 tablespoons coconut oil
- 1 onion, diced
- 2 cloves garlic, minced
- 1 tablespoon ginger, minced
- 2 cups mixed vegetables (carrots, bell peppers, zucchini)
- 1 can (14 oz) coconut milk
- 2 tablespoons curry powder
- Salt to taste
- Fresh cilantro for garnish

Instructions

1. In a large pot, heat coconut oil over medium heat. Sauté onion, garlic, and ginger until softened.
2. Add mixed vegetables and curry powder, cooking for 5 minutes.
3. Pour in coconut milk and simmer for 15-20 minutes until vegetables are tender. Season with salt.
4. Serve warm, garnished with fresh cilantro.

Zucchini and Corn Fritters

Ingredients

- 2 medium zucchinis, grated
- 1 cup corn (fresh or frozen)
- ½ cup all-purpose flour
- 2 large eggs
- ¼ cup green onions, chopped
- ½ teaspoon baking powder
- Salt and pepper to taste
- Olive oil for frying

Instructions

1. In a bowl, mix grated zucchini, corn, flour, eggs, green onions, baking powder, salt, and pepper.
2. Heat olive oil in a skillet over medium heat. Drop spoonfuls of the mixture into the skillet, flattening slightly.
3. Cook for 3-4 minutes on each side until golden brown. Drain on paper towels before serving.

Pomegranate Glazed Brussels Sprouts

Ingredients

- 1 lb Brussels sprouts, halved
- 2 tablespoons olive oil
- Salt and pepper to taste
- ½ cup pomegranate seeds
- ¼ cup balsamic vinegar
- 2 tablespoons honey

Instructions

1. Preheat oven to 400°F (200°C). Toss Brussels sprouts with olive oil, salt, and pepper, and spread them on a baking sheet.
2. Roast for 20-25 minutes until caramelized and tender.
3. In a small saucepan, combine balsamic vinegar and honey, bringing to a simmer until slightly thickened.
4. Drizzle the glaze over roasted Brussels sprouts and toss with pomegranate seeds. Serve warm.

Autumn Harvest Tacos

Ingredients

- 8 corn tortillas
- 1 cup roasted sweet potatoes, cubed
- 1 cup black beans, drained and rinsed
- ½ cup corn (fresh or frozen)
- 1 avocado, sliced
- ¼ cup feta cheese, crumbled (optional)
- 1 teaspoon cumin
- Salt and pepper to taste
- Fresh cilantro for garnish

Instructions

1. In a bowl, combine roasted sweet potatoes, black beans, corn, cumin, salt, and pepper.
2. Warm corn tortillas in a skillet or microwave.
3. Assemble tacos by placing the mixture on each tortilla, topping with avocado, feta, and cilantro. Serve immediately.

Gingerbread Pancakes

Ingredients

- 1 cup all-purpose flour
- 2 tablespoons brown sugar
- 1 teaspoon baking powder
- ½ teaspoon baking soda
- 1 teaspoon ginger
- 1 teaspoon cinnamon
- ¼ teaspoon nutmeg
- ¼ teaspoon salt
- 1 cup buttermilk
- 1 large egg
- 2 tablespoons molasses
- 2 tablespoons melted butter

Instructions

1. In a large bowl, whisk together flour, brown sugar, baking powder, baking soda, ginger, cinnamon, nutmeg, and salt.
2. In another bowl, mix buttermilk, egg, molasses, and melted butter. Combine wet and dry ingredients until just mixed.
3. Heat a non-stick skillet over medium heat. Pour ¼ cup of batter for each pancake, cooking until bubbles form, then flip and cook until golden. Serve with syrup.

Spiced Roasted Cauliflower

Ingredients

- 1 head cauliflower, cut into florets
- 2 tablespoons olive oil
- 1 teaspoon cumin
- 1 teaspoon paprika
- 1 teaspoon garlic powder
- Salt and pepper to taste
- Fresh parsley for garnish

Instructions

1. Preheat oven to 425°F (220°C). Toss cauliflower florets with olive oil, cumin, paprika, garlic powder, salt, and pepper.
2. Spread on a baking sheet and roast for 25-30 minutes until golden and tender.
3. Garnish with fresh parsley before serving.

Creamy Mushroom Soup

Ingredients

- 2 cups mushrooms, sliced
- 1 onion, diced
- 2 cloves garlic, minced
- 4 cups vegetable broth
- 1 cup heavy cream
- 2 tablespoons olive oil
- 1 tablespoon thyme
- Salt and pepper to taste

Instructions

1. In a pot, heat olive oil over medium heat. Sauté onion and garlic until softened.
2. Add mushrooms and thyme, cooking until mushrooms are browned.
3. Pour in vegetable broth and bring to a simmer for 15 minutes.
4. Blend until smooth, then stir in heavy cream. Season with salt and pepper, and serve warm.

Nutty Granola Bars

Ingredients

- 2 cups rolled oats
- ½ cup almond butter
- ½ cup honey or maple syrup
- 1 cup mixed nuts (almonds, walnuts, pecans), chopped
- ½ cup dried fruit (cranberries, apricots, etc.)
- 1 teaspoon vanilla extract
- Pinch of salt

Instructions

1. Preheat oven to 350°F (175°C). Line an 8x8 inch baking dish with parchment paper.
2. In a bowl, mix oats, almond butter, honey, nuts, dried fruit, vanilla, and salt until well combined.
3. Press the mixture into the prepared baking dish. Bake for 20-25 minutes until golden.
4. Allow to cool completely before cutting into bars.

Harvest Vegetable Curry

Ingredients

- 2 tablespoons coconut oil
- 1 onion, diced
- 2 cloves garlic, minced
- 1 tablespoon ginger, minced
- 2 cups mixed vegetables (carrots, bell peppers, zucchini)
- 1 can (14 oz) coconut milk
- 2 tablespoons curry powder
- Salt to taste
- Fresh cilantro for garnish

Instructions

1. In a large pot, heat coconut oil over medium heat. Sauté onion, garlic, and ginger until softened.
2. Add mixed vegetables and curry powder, cooking for 5 minutes.
3. Pour in coconut milk and simmer for 15-20 minutes until vegetables are tender. Season with salt.
4. Serve warm, garnished with fresh cilantro.

Zucchini and Corn Fritters

Ingredients

- 2 medium zucchinis, grated
- 1 cup corn (fresh or frozen)
- ½ cup all-purpose flour
- 2 large eggs
- ¼ cup green onions, chopped
- ½ teaspoon baking powder
- Salt and pepper to taste
- Olive oil for frying

Instructions

1. In a bowl, mix grated zucchini, corn, flour, eggs, green onions, baking powder, salt, and pepper.
2. Heat olive oil in a skillet over medium heat. Drop spoonfuls of the mixture into the skillet, flattening slightly.
3. Cook for 3-4 minutes on each side until golden brown. Drain on paper towels before serving.

Pumpkin Pancakes

Ingredients

- 1 cup all-purpose flour
- 2 tablespoons brown sugar
- 1 teaspoon baking powder
- ½ teaspoon baking soda
- 1 teaspoon cinnamon
- ¼ teaspoon nutmeg
- ¼ teaspoon salt
- 1 cup buttermilk
- 1 large egg
- ½ cup pumpkin puree
- 2 tablespoons melted butter

Instructions

1. In a large bowl, whisk together flour, brown sugar, baking powder, baking soda, cinnamon, nutmeg, and salt.
2. In another bowl, mix buttermilk, egg, pumpkin puree, and melted butter. Combine wet and dry ingredients until just mixed.
3. Heat a non-stick skillet over medium heat. Pour ¼ cup of batter for each pancake, cooking until bubbles form, then flip and cook until golden. Serve with maple syrup.

Carrot Cake Muffins

Ingredients

- 1 ½ cups all-purpose flour
- 1 teaspoon baking soda
- 1 teaspoon baking powder
- 1 teaspoon cinnamon
- ½ teaspoon nutmeg
- ½ teaspoon salt
- 1 cup sugar
- 2 large eggs
- 1 cup grated carrots
- ½ cup vegetable oil
- ½ cup walnuts or raisins (optional)

Instructions

1. Preheat oven to 350°F (175°C). Line a muffin tin with paper liners.
2. In a bowl, mix flour, baking soda, baking powder, cinnamon, nutmeg, and salt.
3. In another bowl, whisk together sugar, eggs, grated carrots, and vegetable oil. Add dry ingredients and mix until just combined. Fold in walnuts or raisins if using.
4. Fill muffin cups ¾ full and bake for 18-20 minutes until a toothpick comes out clean.

Roasted Fennel and Citrus Salad

Ingredients

- 2 bulbs fennel, sliced
- 2 oranges, segmented
- 2 cups arugula or mixed greens
- 2 tablespoons olive oil
- 1 tablespoon balsamic vinegar
- Salt and pepper to taste
- Parmesan cheese shavings for garnish (optional)

Instructions

1. Preheat oven to 400°F (200°C). Toss fennel slices with olive oil, salt, and pepper. Spread on a baking sheet and roast for 25-30 minutes until tender and caramelized.
2. In a large bowl, combine roasted fennel, orange segments, and arugula.
3. Drizzle with balsamic vinegar and toss gently. Garnish with Parmesan shavings before serving.

Harvest Quinoa Salad

Ingredients

- 1 cup quinoa, rinsed and cooked
- 1 cup roasted butternut squash, cubed
- 1 cup cooked black beans, drained and rinsed
- ½ cup pomegranate seeds
- ¼ cup chopped green onions
- ¼ cup feta cheese, crumbled (optional)
- 2 tablespoons olive oil
- 1 tablespoon apple cider vinegar
- Salt and pepper to taste

Instructions

1. In a large bowl, combine cooked quinoa, butternut squash, black beans, pomegranate seeds, green onions, and feta cheese if using.
2. In a small bowl, whisk together olive oil, apple cider vinegar, salt, and pepper. Drizzle over the salad and toss gently. Serve chilled or at room temperature.

Mulled Apple Cider

Ingredients

- 1 gallon apple cider
- 1 orange, sliced
- 5-6 whole cloves
- 2-3 cinnamon sticks
- 1 star anise (optional)
- ½ teaspoon nutmeg

Instructions

1. In a large pot, combine apple cider, orange slices, cloves, cinnamon sticks, star anise, and nutmeg.
2. Heat over medium-low until warm, then reduce to low and simmer for at least 30 minutes to let the flavors meld.
3. Strain and serve warm, garnished with additional orange slices or cinnamon sticks if desired.

Sweet Potato Casserole

Ingredients

- 4 cups mashed sweet potatoes (about 4 large)
- ½ cup brown sugar
- ½ cup milk
- 1 teaspoon vanilla extract
- 2 large eggs
- 1 teaspoon cinnamon
- ½ teaspoon nutmeg
- Topping: 1 cup pecans, chopped, mixed with ½ cup brown sugar and ¼ cup melted butter

Instructions

1. Preheat oven to 350°F (175°C). In a large bowl, combine mashed sweet potatoes, brown sugar, milk, vanilla, eggs, cinnamon, and nutmeg.
2. Transfer the mixture to a greased baking dish and spread evenly.
3. In a separate bowl, mix chopped pecans, brown sugar, and melted butter for the topping. Sprinkle over the sweet potato mixture.
4. Bake for 30-35 minutes until heated through and topping is golden.

Spaghetti Squash Primavera

Ingredients

- 1 medium spaghetti squash
- 2 tablespoons olive oil
- 1 bell pepper, diced
- 1 zucchini, sliced
- 1 cup cherry tomatoes, halved
- 2 cloves garlic, minced
- 1 teaspoon Italian seasoning
- Salt and pepper to taste
- Parmesan cheese for serving (optional)

Instructions

1. Preheat oven to 400°F (200°C). Cut the spaghetti squash in half and remove seeds. Drizzle with olive oil and season with salt and pepper. Place cut side down on a baking sheet and roast for 30-40 minutes until tender.
2. In a skillet, heat olive oil over medium heat. Sauté bell pepper, zucchini, and garlic until tender. Add cherry tomatoes and Italian seasoning, cooking until tomatoes are soft.
3. Once the squash is done, scrape the flesh with a fork to create spaghetti-like strands. Toss with the vegetable mixture and serve warm, topped with Parmesan if desired.

Maple Pecan Granola

Ingredients

- 3 cups rolled oats
- 1 cup pecans, chopped
- ½ cup maple syrup
- ¼ cup vegetable oil
- ½ teaspoon cinnamon
- Pinch of salt
- ½ cup dried fruit (raisins, cranberries, etc.)

Instructions

1. Preheat oven to 350°F (175°C). In a large bowl, combine oats, pecans, maple syrup, vegetable oil, cinnamon, and salt.
2. Spread the mixture on a baking sheet in an even layer. Bake for 20-25 minutes, stirring halfway through, until golden and fragrant.
3. Remove from the oven and let cool completely. Stir in dried fruit and store in an airtight container.

Pumpkin Seed Pesto

Ingredients

- 1 cup pumpkin seeds (pepitas)
- 1 cup fresh basil leaves
- 2 cloves garlic
- ½ cup grated Parmesan cheese
- ½ cup olive oil
- Salt and pepper to taste
- Juice of ½ lemon

Instructions

1. In a food processor, combine pumpkin seeds, basil, garlic, and Parmesan cheese. Pulse until finely chopped.
2. With the processor running, slowly drizzle in olive oil until smooth.
3. Season with salt, pepper, and lemon juice. Blend again to combine. Serve with pasta, bread, or as a dip.

Chocolate Chip Pumpkin Bread

Ingredients

- 1 ½ cups all-purpose flour
- 1 teaspoon baking soda
- ½ teaspoon baking powder
- ½ teaspoon salt
- 1 teaspoon cinnamon
- ½ teaspoon nutmeg
- 1 cup sugar
- ½ cup vegetable oil
- 1 cup pumpkin puree
- 2 large eggs
- 1 teaspoon vanilla extract
- ¾ cup chocolate chips

Instructions

1. Preheat oven to 350°F (175°C). Grease a loaf pan.
2. In a bowl, whisk together flour, baking soda, baking powder, salt, cinnamon, and nutmeg.
3. In another bowl, mix sugar, vegetable oil, pumpkin puree, eggs, and vanilla until smooth. Combine wet and dry ingredients, then fold in chocolate chips.
4. Pour batter into the prepared pan and bake for 50-60 minutes, until a toothpick comes out clean. Let cool before slicing.

Roasted Garlic and Rosemary Mashed Potatoes

Ingredients

- 2 lbs potatoes, peeled and cubed
- 1 head garlic
- ½ cup milk
- ¼ cup butter, softened
- 1 tablespoon fresh rosemary, chopped
- Salt and pepper to taste

Instructions

1. Preheat oven to 400°F (200°C). Slice the top off the garlic head, drizzle with olive oil, and wrap in foil. Roast for 30-35 minutes until soft.
2. Boil potatoes in salted water until tender. Drain and return to the pot.
3. Squeeze roasted garlic into the potatoes and add milk, butter, rosemary, salt, and pepper. Mash until smooth and creamy. Serve warm.

Acorn Squash and Wild Rice Soup

Ingredients

- 1 medium acorn squash, peeled and cubed
- 1 cup wild rice, cooked
- 1 onion, diced
- 2 carrots, diced
- 2 celery stalks, diced
- 3 cloves garlic, minced
- 4 cups vegetable broth
- 1 teaspoon thyme
- Salt and pepper to taste
- 2 tablespoons olive oil

Instructions

1. In a large pot, heat olive oil over medium heat. Sauté onion, carrots, and celery until softened. Add garlic and thyme, cooking for another minute.
2. Add acorn squash and vegetable broth. Bring to a boil, then reduce heat and simmer for 20-25 minutes until squash is tender.
3. Use an immersion blender to blend the soup until smooth, then stir in cooked wild rice. Season with salt and pepper before serving.

Honeycrisp Apple Salad

Ingredients

- 4 cups mixed greens
- 2 Honeycrisp apples, thinly sliced
- ½ cup walnuts, toasted
- ½ cup feta cheese, crumbled
- ¼ cup dried cranberries
- 2 tablespoons olive oil
- 1 tablespoon apple cider vinegar
- Salt and pepper to taste

Instructions

1. In a large bowl, combine mixed greens, sliced apples, walnuts, feta, and cranberries.
2. In a small bowl, whisk together olive oil, apple cider vinegar, salt, and pepper. Drizzle over the salad and toss gently. Serve immediately.

Maple Dijon Glazed Salmon

Ingredients

- 4 salmon fillets
- ¼ cup maple syrup
- 2 tablespoons Dijon mustard
- 1 tablespoon soy sauce
- Salt and pepper to taste
- Lemon wedges for serving (optional)

Instructions

1. Preheat oven to 400°F (200°C). Line a baking sheet with parchment paper.
2. In a small bowl, whisk together maple syrup, Dijon mustard, soy sauce, salt, and pepper.
3. Place salmon fillets on the baking sheet and brush with the maple glaze. Bake for 12-15 minutes, until the salmon is cooked through and flakes easily. Serve with lemon wedges if desired.

Chocolate Hazelnut Spread with Apples

Ingredients

- 1 cup hazelnuts, toasted
- ½ cup dark chocolate, melted
- 2 tablespoons cocoa powder
- 2 tablespoons maple syrup or honey
- 1 teaspoon vanilla extract
- Apples, sliced for serving

Instructions

1. In a food processor, blend toasted hazelnuts until smooth and creamy.
2. Add melted chocolate, cocoa powder, maple syrup, and vanilla extract. Blend until well combined and smooth.
3. Serve with sliced apples for dipping.

Printed in the USA
CPSIA information can be obtained
at www.ICGtesting.com
LVHW081745291024
795101LV00011B/304

9 798330 448555